D0598299

Gareth Stevens Publishing
A WORLD ALMANAC EDUCATION GROUP COMPANY

Written by
DORA YIP/MARK CRAMER

Designed by
LYNN CHIN

Picture research by
SUSAN JANE MANUEL

First published in North America in 2001 by
Gareth Stevens Publishing
A World Almanac Education Group Company
330 West Olive Street, Suite 100
Milwaukee, Wisconsin 53212 USA

For a free color catalog describing
Gareth Stevens' list of high-quality books
and multimedia programs, call
1-800-542-2595 (USA) or
1-800-461-9120 (CANADA).
Gareth Stevens Publishing's
Fax: (414) 332-3567.

Originated and designed by
Times Editions
An imprint of Times Media Private Limited
A member of the Times Publishing Group
Times Centre, 1 New Industrial Road
Singapore 536196
http://www.timesone.com.sg/te

Library of Congress Cataloging-in-Publication Data
available upon request from the publisher.
Fax: (414) 336-0157 for the attention of the
Publishing Records Department.

ISBN 0-8368-2516-0

Printed in Malaysia

1 2 3 4 5 6 7 8 9 05 04 03 02 01

PICTURE CREDITS

A.N.A. Press Agency: 4, 5, 31, 37
Archive Photos: 15 (bottom)
John Denham: 35
HBL Network Photo Agency: 13, 15 (center), 17 (both), 18 (both), 21, 41
Hutchison Library: 23
International Photobank: 2, 16, 33
Bjorn Klingwall: 8, 19, 24, 25, 29, 32
Earl and Nazima Kowall: 3 (top), 38
North Wind Picture Archives: 10, 11 (both)
Christine Osborne: 7, 26, 28, 40
David Simson: 1, 9 (top), 20, 30, 45
South American Pictures: cover, 3 (bottom), 6, 9 (bottom), 12, 15 (top), 22, 27, 34, 36, 39
Liba Taylor: 14
Nik Wheeler: 3 (center)

Digital Scanning by Superskill Graphics Pte Ltd

Contents

Words that appear in the glossary are printed in **boldface** type the first time they occur in the text.

CRECIDOS E
ATALLAS

Welcome to Cuba!

Cuba is a vibrant country that is famous around the world more for its politics than for its unique and rich culture. Cubans are proud of their heritage and the beautiful land they live in. Let's learn more about Cuba and its people!

Opposite: Political rallies are often held in Havana's Plaza de Revolución.

Below: Cubans gather at the José Martí memorial in Havana for the anniversary of the national rebellion led by Fidel Castro in 1953.

The Flag of Cuba

The Cuban flag was officially adopted in 1902. Based on a design by Narciso López, a Spanish Venezuelan, the flag features a red triangle that represents liberty, equality, and **fraternity**. Red symbolizes the blood shed by **revolutionaries**.

The Land

Made up of over 1,600 islands and islets, the Republic of Cuba lies at the **crossroads** of North America, Central America, the Gulf of Mexico, the Caribbean Sea, and the Atlantic Ocean.

Most of the country's people live on the main island of Cuba, which covers an area of 40,519 square miles (104,944 square kilometers), making it the fifteenth largest island in the world.

Below: Famous for its beaches, Cayo Largo forms part of the Los Canarreos **archipelago**.

Above: The Sierra Maestra is the longest mountain range in Cuba. It is more than 100 miles (161 km) long. It is also the source of the Cauto River.

Cuba has some of the world's most spectacular beaches, but **rural** Cubans, called *guajiros* (gwa-HEE-rohs), prefer the green mountains of the interior. The province of Pinar del Río has unique flat-topped mountains, called *mogotes* (moh-GOH-tehs). This kind of mountain is found only in Cuba.

The Cauto is the longest river in Cuba. It flows west for 230 miles (370 km) before emptying into the Gulf of Guacanayabo.

Above: The fan-leafed Washingtonia palm is one of Cuba's sixty palm tree species. This tree keeps its dead leaves, which form a "skirt" around the trunk.

Climate and Seasons

Cuba has a tropical climate with two seasons. The wet season lasts from May to October. The dry season lasts from November to April. A tropical hurricane strikes during the wet season every one or two years.

Plants and Animals

Most of Cuba's 8,000 types of tropical plants grow in limited areas because much of the land has been turned into plantations for growing crops. Cuba has many types of palm trees, including the national tree — the royal palm.

A wide variety of animals lives in Cuba, including rare animals, such as the *majá* (ma-HAH), a nonpoisonous python, and the alligator gar, one of the biggest freshwater fish in the world. The tiny bee hummingbird is one of 300 bird species found in Cuba. It is the smallest bird in the world.

Above: Cuba's marshlands are home to the tropical river crab. This rare freshwater creature can breathe both underwater and on land.

Left: A Cuban ground iguana grows up to 4 feet (1.2 meters) in length and can move very quickly.

History

Little is known about the original people of Cuba — the Taino and Ciboney Indians. In the sixteenth century, Spanish **colonists** brought diseases, wars, and hardship that quickly wiped out these native tribes. In the 1700s, the Spanish government brought African slaves to Cuba to work on the sugar plantations.

Below: Havana Bay was one of the busiest harbors in Spain's colonial empire by the 1700s.

Left: The USS *Indiana* was one of the navy ships that fought against the Spanish in the Battle of Santiago, which was the last major battle of the Spanish-American War. The war ended when Spain surrendered the city of Santiago de Cuba to the U.S. on July 17, 1898.

Wars of Independence

The first movement to free Cuba from Spain led to the **abolition** of slavery in 1886. José Martí helped start a second war against the Spanish in 1895. This revolution led to the Spanish-American War in 1898. When Spain lost the war, Cuba became independent. The U.S. military, however, occupied Cuba until 1902, when Tomás Estrada Palma became Cuba's first elected president.

Above: During the Spanish-American War, Theodore Roosevelt led the 1st Volunteer Cavalry, called "the Rough Riders." He became president of the United States in 1901.

U.S. Occupation

Above: Cuba's presidential palace was built in 1922. After the overthrow of Batista in 1959, it was converted into the Museum of the Revolution.

Cuba's freedom came with a price. Cuba had to adopt the Platt Amendment, which allowed the U.S. to **intervene** in its political and economic affairs.

From 1902 to 1959, Cuba was run by **corrupt dictators**, including Fulgencio Batista, who held power from 1933 to 1944. When Batista returned to politics in 1952, he angered many people. One of them was a lawyer named Fidel Castro.

The Cuban Revolution

In 1953, Castro and a group of **rebels** attacked a military base. Castro was caught and sent to prison. Most of the rebels were killed. When Castro was released from prison, in 1955, he formed another group, called the 26th of July Movement, with his brother Raúl and Ernesto "Che" Guevara. For four years, this group used **guerrilla warfare** against Batista's army. Batista finally fled the country on January 1, 1959, and Castro became Cuba's new leader.

Left: Fidel Castro is one of the most important revolutionary figures in history. He became premier, or prime minister, of Cuba in February 1959.

Castro's Cuba

Since 1959, Cuba has become known for its **socialist** policies. When Castro tried to spread these policies to other Latin American countries, the U.S. sent forces to stop him. The Soviet Union stepped in to help Cuba, causing tension between the U.S. and the Soviet Union.

When the Soviet Union collapsed in 1991, Cuba's economy also collapsed. Castro urged Cubans to be **patriotic** through the hard times ahead.

Below: Young Cubans wave their country's flag and cheer during an anniversary celebration of the 1959 revolution.

José Martí (1853–1895)

National hero José Martí led the Cuban independence movement in the late 1800s. He died fighting in the revolution against Spain in 1895.

José Martí

Fidel Castro (c. 1926–)

Head of Cuba's government since 1959, Fidel Castro has remained in control of the country in spite of troubled relations with the U.S. and the collapse of the Soviet Union.

Fidel Castro

Nicolás Guillén (1902–1989)

Regarded as Cuba's national poet, Nicolás Guillén headed Cuba's Union of Writers and Artists after returning from **exile** in 1959.

Nicolás Guillén

María Caridad Colón (1959–)

In the 1980 Olympic Games, Colón, a javelin thrower, became the first woman from a developing country to win a gold medal.

Government and the Economy

Cuba is a socialist republic and has only one official national political party — the Communist Party of Cuba. Fidel Castro became the party's first secretary in 1976.

The government controls the economy, but citizens have the right to elect representatives to government. Made up of 589 elected members, the

Below: The main office for the Cuban Academy of Sciences in Havana was once the National Capitol building.

Left: This political poster reads, "Socialism or death!"

National Assembly of the People's Power is responsible for making laws, and it elects the thirty-one members of the executive State Council. The State Council enforces law and public policy. Castro has been the president of the State Council since 1976.

Cuba is divided into fourteen official provinces, which have their own local assemblies. The government has created several large organizations, such as the Federation of Cuban Women and the Confederation of Cuban Workers, to deal with social and welfare issues.

Above: Camilo Cienfuegos (*left*) and Ernesto Che Guevara (*right*) were Cuban rebels.

Left: Cattle pull a heavy load for a farmer in Viñales, which is in eastern Cuba. This region is well-known for its fertile tobacco fields.

An Independent Economy

Cuba is still struggling with the economic problems that came after the Soviet breakup in 1991. The United States added to those troubles when it tightened its **embargo** against Cuba. Today, Cubans regularly face shortages of food, fuel, and medicine.

Above: This woman is hand-rolling dried tobacco leaves to make a cigar. Tobacco has always played an important role in Cuban society.

Working for the State

In Cuba, people work for the good of the state and not for their own gains.

Laborers earn almost as much as professionals, and a taxi driver might earn more than a doctor.

Major Industries

Tourism is the fastest growing industry in Cuba. Cuban beach resorts attract many visitors, and Havana is a popular place to hold business conventions. Crops, such as sugar cane and tobacco, are also vital to Cuba's economy.

Below: This plant in Moa, in eastern Cuba, produces nickel, which is Cuba's most important mining export.

People and Lifestyle

Since the 1959 revolution, Cuba has become one of the most racially united countries in the world. Cuban children have equal opportunities at school, and many women and **ethnic** minorities hold high-ranking jobs.

Cuba has three main ethnic groups: whites, blacks, and mixed races, known as *mulattoes* (people of mixed black

Left: These Cuban boys belong to different ethnic groups, but they have equal opportunities for education, jobs, and friendships.

and white ancestry) and *mestizos* (people of mixed Spanish and native Indian ancestry). The main minority groups are Jews and Chinese. Many Chinese left Cuba after the 1959 revolution, but Havana still has an active Chinatown.

Above: A Cuban woman stands outside her home in Trinidad, a city in southern central Cuba. Trinidad has a mixed ethnic heritage that comes across through the languages and traditions of the people who live there.

With social class differences and **capitalism** gone, Cuban interests have changed from wanting to make money to wanting to excel in other areas, such as education and athletics.

Family Life

Unlike other Latin American families, most Cuban families do not have more than two children. In most Cuban neighborhoods, however, different families treat each other like relatives, rather than like friends or neighbors.

Below: These young Cuban children live in rural Sierra de los Órganos.

Cuban women are not limited to traditional roles at home. After the 1959 revolution, the government gave women equal opportunities in the workplace. Today, women make up 42 percent of Cuba's workforce. With so many mothers in the workforce, Cuban fathers and children have learned to share the chores at home.

Most Cubans live in small, crowded apartments. In spite of the living conditions, they enjoy some important benefits. The government provides each Cuban with free health care,

free child care, and free education. Cuban students can go on school-sponsored trips to wilderness areas called *campismos* (cahm-PEES-mos). They can also spend time in the countryside helping local farmers.

Above: Three women relax in downtown Havana.

Education

All education is free in Cuba. Children forty-five days to six years old can go to day-care centers. They learn simple skills in reading, mathematics, and science. After a year in kindergarten, children go to elementary school for six grades and junior high school for three grades. Then they start high school.

High school students have to study history, mathematics, biology, physics, and chemistry. Although university

Left: Many Cubans work for the country's education system.

Above: Schoolgirls from the Lenin School in Havana relax between classes. Girls no longer face **discrimination** at school because all Cubans now receive an equal education within a national system.

education is free, students need very good grades in high school to gain admission. The Cuban education system teaches practical and technical skills that will help students find jobs quickly. Some students find jobs even while they are still in school.

Cuban schools offer many after-school activities, such as sports, dances, and volunteer work. Students pay a fee of one Cuban peso (1 CUP), or U.S. $0.05, every month for these activities.

Above: Cathedral San Cristobal de la Habana is a Catholic Church built between 1704 and 1777.

Religion

Cuba has a unique **Afro-Cuban** religion called Santería. It combines West African religious worship with Roman Catholic practices. Santería evolved from the **pagan** religions that African slaves brought to Cuba. Now the country has about 4,000 Santerían priests, and the religion attracts black, mulatto, and white followers.

The main religion of white Cubans is Roman Catholicism. Cuba has 260 Catholic priests, and only two of them are black. Pope John Paul II visited Cuba in 1998.

In the 1960s, the Cuban government discouraged organized religion, and many Catholics, Protestants, and Jews left Cuba. Organized religion is slowly making a comeback, but almost half of the Cuban population is nonreligious.

Below: Onlookers watch a Santerían celebration in the streets of Havana.

Language

All Cubans speak Spanish. Although Spanish and English use the same alphabet, the Spanish language contains two sounds that are not found in English: the "rr," a sound made by fluttering the tongue, and the "j," which sounds like an English "h."

Yoruban, a language introduced by African slaves, is still used by followers of the Santerían religion.

Left: Most bookstores, such as this outdoor bookstall in Havana, sell books either by or about Ernesto "Che" Guevara. Guevara wrote about political events and described fighting in the 1959 revolution.

Above: Cubans have a variety of newspapers and magazines available to them.

Literature

Some of Cuba's greatest national heroes and revolutionaries wrote some of the country's greatest literature. José Martí wrote beautiful poetry about his desire to free Cuba from Spain in the 1880s. Nicolás Guillén explored his African heritage in his poetry. Journalist, diplomat, and **musicologist** Alejo Carpentier is considered Cuba's greatest novelist.

Arts

Cuban artists are fully supported by the government. The National Cultural Council was formed in 1961 to help artists pursue their careers.

Music

Afro-Cuban music has influenced music from rock 'n' roll to jazz all around the world. Salsa is a popular dance music with Afro-Cuban roots.

Below: Street musicians are a common sight in Cuba. Cuban music, like all Cuban arts, has strong African and Spanish influences.

Above: This modern dance troupe is practicing for a performance. Dancing is very important to Cubans. The Modern Dance Company in Havana and the National Folk Company (a folk dancing troupe) are very popular.

Traditional Cuban music includes *Nueva Trova* (new-AY-vah TROH-vah), which mixes poetry with folk songs, and *Punto Guajiro* (POON-toh gwa-HEE-roh), which is Cuban country music.

Dance

In Cuba, music and dancing go together. People of all ages dance to salsa and jazz at music festivals held throughout the year.

Painting and Sculpture

"Naive art" is a popular form of painting in Cuba. Most naive artists do not have formal training. They usually paint bright, colorful scenes of city and country life. Cuba's most famous painter was Wilfredo Lam.

Sculpture is also a popular art form in Cuba. Cuban sculptors use typical materials, such as wood, marble, and metal, but they also use local materials, such as coconuts and snail shells.

Above: A Cuban artist paints scenes of the Cuban countryside in his Santiago studio.

Twice a year, Cuba holds the Havana Biennial, an international festival that displays art from developing countries.

Film

Filmmakers from around the world study at the Cuban Institute of Cinematographic Art and Industry. Cuba's most famous director was Tomás Gutiérrez Alea (1928–1996), whose films were often funny, romantic, and **satirical**.

Left: The National Theater is one of Cuba's most beautiful buildings. It is located on the Prado, an avenue in Old Havana. This theater, also known as García Lorca Theater, was named after Spanish poet Federico García Lorca.

Leisure

Cubans are very sociable. Almost all of their leisure activities, from watching television to eating meals, involve groups of people. Families leave their front doors open on weekends, and neighbors walk in and out freely.

People often gather in public parks or even on street corners to relax and chat with friends. In Havana, a favorite

Below: Tourists visiting a Havana bar enjoy the openness of Cuban social life.

gathering place is the *Malécon* (mah-leh-CONE). It is a stone wall that protects the north side of the city from the pounding waves of the sea.

Above: Games, such as chess, are popular in Cuba, especially among adults and teenagers.

"The Era of the Bicycle"

Bicycle riding has always been popular in Cuba, but oil shortages after the 1991 Soviet breakup made it necessary. The government even gave free bicycles to all Cubans who did not own one.

Above: Basketball is a popular playground sport for Cuban schoolchildren.

Sports

In 1961, when the Cuban government founded the National Institute of Sports, all Cubans gained free or low-cost entry to sports facilities and events. Cubans particularly enjoy baseball, softball, basketball, and volleyball.

Baseball is Cuba's most popular sport. The Cuban baseball league is one of the best in the world. In 1996, the Cuban national baseball team won an Olympic gold medal.

Cuba sponsors national sports tournaments in cross-country cycling, fencing, track and field, and boxing.

One of Cuba's sports legends is boxer Teófilo Stevenson. He was the first boxer to win three Olympic gold medals at three Olympic Games in a row. Stevenson has been offered millions of dollars to box in the United States, but he has chosen to stay in Cuba. He has become a role model for other Cuban athletes to stay in Cuba.

Below: Olympic gold-medal boxer Teófilo Stevenson (*center*) makes many public appearances. He encourages young Cubans to take part in national sporting events, such as the Havana Marathon.

Festivals

Carnaval is Cuba's biggest, oldest, and most important festival. From late July to early August, dancers parade through the streets, and music and parties go on for days. Some Cuban music festivals, such as the Havana International Jazz Festival, are famous throughout the world.

A religious festival, Romería de Mayo (the May pilgrimage), is held every year in Holguín, a city in eastern

Below: Cuban celebrations, such as Carnaval, always include gaily dressed dancers.

Left: Young Santeríans celebrate their African, Cuban, and Spanish heritage during a festival.

Cuba. During the first week in May, pilgrims climb the Loma de la Cruz (Hill of the Cross) to visit a cross placed there by the Spanish in the 1700s.

Christmastime is special in the town of Remedios. On the last Saturday of the year, the town has a contest for the most elaborate *carrozas* (cah-RROH-sahs), or parade floats.

Food

The Cuban diet changed in the 1990s, when Cuba lost some of its trading partners. Cuban farmers suddenly had to provide the country's food supply. The government introduced two vegetables, sweet potatoes and ***yuca*** (YOO-cah), to replace imported rice and wheat. Cuban dishes are usually less spicy than the foods of other Latin American countries.

Below: A Cuban buys pork at a Chinese butcher's stall. Pork is a common food in the Cuban diet. It is the main ingredient in one of Cuba's most prized dishes, ***lechón*** **(leh-CHONE), which is roast pig flavored with bitter orange and garlic.**

Above: An El Rápido waitress serves fast food — on roller skates! El Rápido is one of only a few fast-food restaurants in Cuba. El Rápido restaurants are owned by the government. They mainly serve hot dogs and hamburgers.

Rations and Restaurants

The Cuban government provides some food products at low prices through a monthly **rationing** system. Food rations, however, do not last the whole month, so most Cubans have a vegetable garden or have to spend money to buy more food.

Since the mid-1990s, small private restaurants, called *paladares* (pah-lah-DAR-ehs), have been allowed in Cuba. They serve home-cooked food.

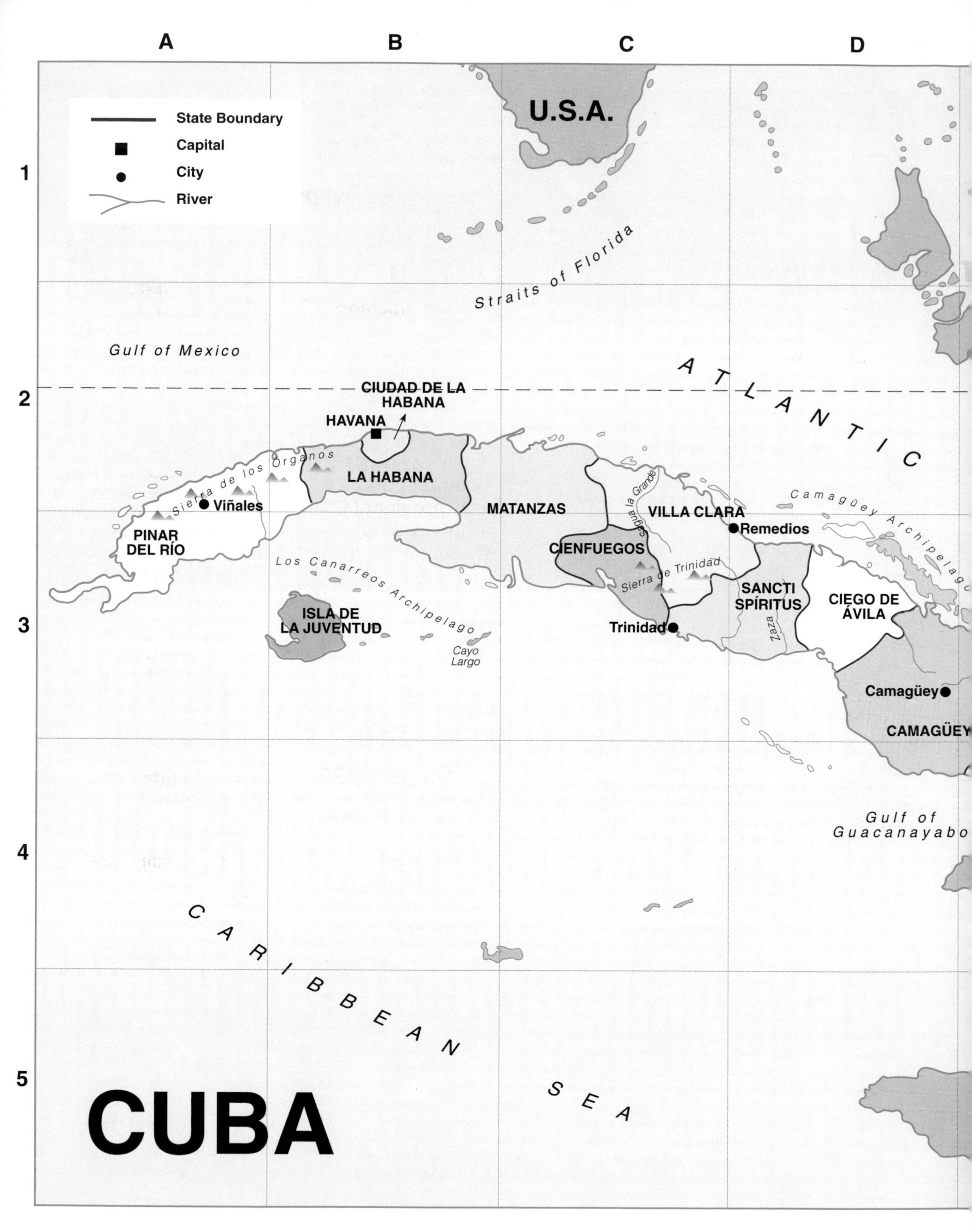
A
B
C
D
1
2
3
4
5
State Boundary
Capital
City
River
U.S.A.
Straits of Florida
Gulf of Mexico
ATLANTIC
CIUDAD DE LA HABANA
HAVANA
LA HABANA
Sierra de los Órganos
Viñales
PINAR DEL RÍO
MATANZAS
Sagua la Grande
VILLA CLARA
Remedios
Camagüey Archipelago
CIENFUEGOS
Sierra de Trinidad
Los Canarreos Archipelago
ISLA DE LA JUVENTUD
Cayo Largo
Trinidad
SANCTI SPÍRITUS
Zaza
CIEGO DE ÁVILA
Camagüey
CAMAGÜEY
Gulf of Guacanayabo
CARIBBEAN SEA
CUBA

E
F
N
THE BAHAMAS
Tropic of Cancer
OCEAN
LAS TUNAS
Holguín
HOLGUÍN
Moa
Cauto
Bayamo
GRANMA
SANTIAGO DE CUBA
GUANTÁNAMO
Sierra Maestra
Guantánamo
Santiago de Cuba
Pico Turquino (6,561 feet/2,000 m)

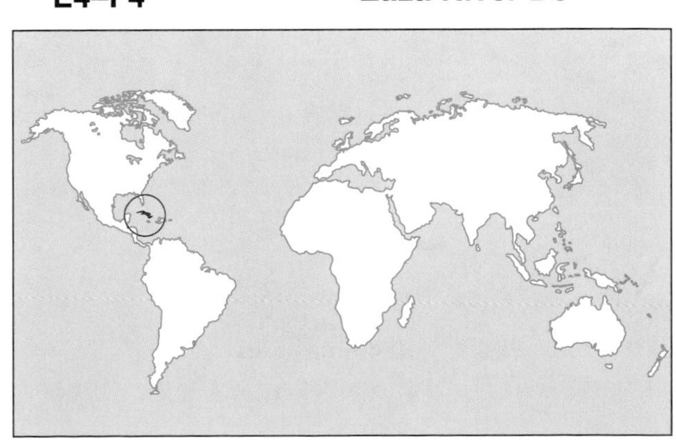

Quick Facts

Official Name República de Cuba, Republic of Cuba

Capital Havana

Official Language Spanish

Population 11,096,395 (July 1999 estimate)

Land Area 42,804 square miles (110,862 square km)

Provinces Camagüey, Ciego de Avila, Cienfuegos, Ciudad de La Habana, Granma, Guantánamo, Holguín, La Habana, Las Tunas, Matanzas, Pinar del Río, Sancti Spíritus, Santiago de Cuba, Villa Clara

Major Cities Bayamo, Camagüey, Guantánamo, Holguín, Santiago de Cuba

Major Mountains Sierra Maestra, Sierra de los Órganos, Sierra de Trinidad

Highest Point Pico Turquino 6,561 feet (2,000 m)

Major Rivers Cauto, Sagua la Grande, Zaza

Main Imports Fossil fuels, food products, machinery, chemicals

Main Exports Sugar, minerals, fish, tobacco products, citrus fruits

Currency Cuban peso (CUP 21 = U.S. $1 in 2000)

Opposite: Cuban souvenirs are extremely popular with tourists.

Alegre
cuba
cuba
SOUVENIR
¡NOW
PHOTO
LA B DEL M
50
Capri
hotel
INTUR/CUBA
hotel
Capri
HABANA
RIO
HAWAII
USA
Benny More
HOTEL
St. John's
HNC
SOUVENIR
Cuba
¡NOW
.cuba-love.
cuba
COHIBA
the sun's
favorite beach
Varadero
INTUR/CUBA
cuba
cuba
1830
Alegre

Glossary

abolition: the formal ending of something, such as slavery.

Afro-Cuban: referring to the Cuban culture that has African heritage.

archipelago: a chain of islands.

capitalism: an economic system in which private individuals or companies control the production and distribution of goods and services.

colonists: people who settle in an area, often taking that area from another group of people.

corrupt: willing to be dishonest or do something illegal in return for money.

crossroads: a place where two or more paths cross each other.

dictators: rulers who have complete authority over a country.

discrimination: the practice of treating a person or a group less fairly than other people or groups.

embargo: a government order that does not allow the buying and selling of goods with another country.

ethnic: relating to a certain race or culture of people.

exile: the state of being sent away by force from a person's native land.

fraternity: the quality of caring for other people as if they were family members.

guerrilla warfare: the use of surprise attacks by small groups of soldiers to fight a much larger enemy force.

intervene: to step in.

musicologist: a person who studies music for knowledge instead of to perform.

pagan: having little or no religion, or worshiping material goods or many gods.

patriotic: loyal to one's country.

rationing: dividing small supplies of goods among large numbers of people.

rebels: people who fight against some kind of controlling authority.

revolutionaries: people who begin or support a political revolution.

rural: related to the countryside.

satirical: characterized by wit or irony to make fun of something in a bitter way.

socialist: relating to a political system in which the government owns and controls the country's economy.

***yuca* (YOO-cah):** a tropical plant with a root that is starchy and can be eaten.

More Books to Read

Child of the Sun: A Cuban Legend. Legends of the World series. Sandra Martin Arnold (Troll)

Children of Cuba. Frank Staub (Carolrhoda Books)

Cuba. Major World Nations series. Clifford W. Crouch (Chelsea House)

Cuba: After the Revolution. Bernard Wolf (Dutton Books)

Cuba: City and Village Life. Country Insights series. Marion Morrison (Raintree/Steck-Vaughn)

Cubans in America. The in America series. Adriana Mendez Rodenas (Lerner)

José Martí: Man of Poetry, Soldier of Freedom. Hispanic Heritage series. Alan West (Millbrook Press)

The Life and Times of Fidel Castro. Esther Selsdon (Chelsea House)

Los Zapaticos de Rosa. José Martí (Lectorum)

Under the Royal Palms: A Childhood in Cuba. Alma Flor Ada (Atheneum)

Videos

Cuba. On Top of the World series. (Superior Home Video)

El Che: Investigating a Legend. (Kultur Video)

Fidel Castro. A & E Biography series. (A & E Entertainment)

Hemingway in Cuba. (Kultur Video)

Web Sites

www.cuba.com

www.cubaweb.cu/pueblo/people.html

www.sims.berkeley.edu/~lcush/CPP.htm

www.virtourist.com/america/pinardelrio

Due to the dynamic nature of the Internet, some web sites stay current longer than others. To find additional web sites, use a reliable search engine with one or more of the following keywords to help you locate information about Cuba. Keywords: *Fidel Castro, Cubans, Ernesto "Che" Guevara, Havana, Malecón, salsa.*

Index